D0122743

Mayflies

The Beautiful Changes and Other Poems
Ceremony and Other Poems
A Bestiary (editor, with Alexander Calder)
Molière's *The Misanthrope* (translator)
Things of This World
Poems 1943–1956
Candide (with Lillian Hellman)
Poe: Complete Poems (editor)
Advice to a Prophet and Other Poems
Molière's *Tartuffe* (translator)
The Poems of Richard Wilbur
Loudmouse (for children)
Shakespeare: Poems (co-editor, with Alfred Harbage)
Walking to Sleep: New Poems and Translations
Molière's *The School for Wives* (translator)
Opposites
The Mind-Reader: New Poems
Responses: Prose Pieces, 1948–1976
Molière's *The Learned Ladies* (translator)
Racine's *Andromache* (translator)
Racine's *Phaedra* (translator)
New and Collected Poems
More Opposites
The Catbird's Song: Prose Pieces 1963–1995

Mayflies

New Poems and Translations

RICHARD WILBUR

HARCOURT, INC. *New York   San Diego   London*

"The Albatross" and "Correspondences" by Charles Baudelaire, translated
by Richard Wilbur, from *The Flowers of Evil,* copyright © 1965 by New
Directions Publishing Corp. Reprinted by permission of New Directions
Publishing Corp.

Canto XXV from Dante's *Inferno* originally published in Daniel Halpern's
Dante's Inferno: Translations by Twenty Contemporary Poets © 1993 by Ecco
Press and HarperCollins. Reprinted by permission of HarperCollins.

"A Cry from Childhood" by Valeri Petrov first published in *Window on
the Black Sea* © 1992 Carnegie-Mellon Press. Reprinted by permission of
Carnegie-Mellon Press.

Library of Congress Cataloging-in-Publication Data
Wilbur, Richard, 1921–
Mayflies:new poems and translations/Richard Wilbur.—1st ed.
p.   cm.
ISBN 0-15-100469-2
I. Title
PS3545.I32165 M39   2000
811'.52 21—dc21   99-045452

Text set in Granjon
Design by Ivan Holmes

Printed in the United States of America
First edition
J I H G F E D C B A

Some of these poems have appeared in the *New Yorker,* the *Sewanee Theological Review, 21st,* the *New Republic,* the *Epigrammatist,* the *Atlantic Monthly,* the *Carolina Review,* the *Oxford American, Image,* the *Yale Review,* the *Paris Review,* and the *New York Review of Books.* The Ecco Press first published the Dante canto in its edition of the *Inferno* (1993), and the complete translation of Molière's *Amphitryon* was brought out by Harcourt Brace in 1995. Slightly different earlier versions of the Baudelaire translations first appeared in Marthiel and Jackson Mathews's edition of *The Flowers of Evil* (New Directions, 1955).

For my daughter Ellen

Contents

TRANSFORMATIONS

Mayflies

Changes

A Barred Owl

The warping night air having brought the boom
Of an owl's voice into her darkened room,
We tell the wakened child that all she heard
Was an odd question from a forest bird,
Asking of us, if rightly listened to,
"Who cooks for you?" and then "Who cooks for you?"

Words, which can make our terrors bravely clear,
Can also thus domesticate a fear,
And send a small child back to sleep at night
Not listening for the sound of stealthy flight
Or dreaming of some small thing in a claw
Borne up to some dark branch and eaten raw.

For C.

After the clash of elevator gates
And the long sinking, she emerges where,
A slight thing in the morning's crosstown glare,
She looks up toward the window where he waits,
Then in a fleeting taxi joins the rest
Of the huge traffic bound forever west.

On such grand scale do lovers say good-bye—
Even this other pair whose high romance
Had only the duration of a dance,
And who, now taking leave with stricken eye,
See each in each a whole new life forgone.
For them, above the darkling clubhouse lawn,

Bright Perseids flash and crumble; while for these
Who part now on the dock, weighed down by grief
And baggage, yet with something like relief,
It takes three thousand miles of knitting seas
To cancel out their crossing, and unmake
The amorous rough and tumble of their wake.

We are denied, my love, their fine tristesse
And bittersweet regrets, and cannot share
The frequent vistas of their large despair,
Where love and all are swept to nothingness;
Still, there's a certain scope in that long love
Which constant spirits are the keepers of,

And which, though taken to be tame and staid,
Is a wild sostenuto of the heart,
A passion joined to courtesy and art
Which has the quality of something made,
Like a good fiddle, like the rose's scent,
Like a rose window or the firmament.

Zea

see p. 77

Once their fruit is picked,
The cornstalks lighten, and though
Keeping to their strict

Rows, begin to be
The tall grasses that they are—
Lissom, now, and free

As canes that clatter
In island wind, or plumed reeds
Rocked by lake water.

Soon, if not cut down,
Their ranks grow whistling-dry, and
Blanch to lightest brown,

So that, one day, all
Their ribbon-like, down-arcing
Leaves rise up and fall

In tossed companies,
Like goose-wings beating southward
Over the changed trees.

Later, there are days
Full of bare expectancy,
Downcast hues, and haze,

Days of an utter
Calm, in which one white corn-leaf,
Oddly aflutter,

Its fabric sheathing
A gaunt stem, can seem to be
The sole thing breathing.

At Moorditch

see p. 77

"Now," said the voice of lock and window-bar,
"You must confront things as they truly are.
      Open your eyes at last, and see
The desolateness of reality."

"Things have," I said, "a pallid, empty look,
Like pictures in an unused coloring book."

"Now that the scales have fallen from your eyes,"
Said the sad hallways, "you must recognize
      How childishly your former sight
Salted the world with glory and delight."

"This cannot be the world," I said. "Nor will it,
Till the heart's crayon spangle and fulfill it."

Bonds

1

The bully focuses the coward's fears;
The grateful coward weeps the bully's tears.

2

The reader's tyrannous desires compel
The weary, bored pornographer to tell
Again, and then once more, and then anew,
The shameful things that lustful monsters do
To a blameless victim—chained, or drugged, or tied—
With whom the reader feels identified.

The Gambler

Full of a cold excitement, he betrays
      His creditors and all he loves
With long-shot wagers, till at length he shoves
A last few chips across the glowing baize.

It thrills him to be almost free of hope.
      The tossed white ball begins to strike
The spinning wheel-compartments, sounding like
The stutter of a stretching gallows-rope.

Still, not until the ball has come to rest
      Will he be able to achieve
A pure despair. Meanwhile he must believe
As best he can in luck, which at its best

Affects him as a love both great and grim—
      A love whose boyish pet he is,
A love of prodigal indulgences,
Doting, divine, and cold to all but him.

Three Tankas

ON LYMAN FLAT

Scattered raindrops fall
On the roadside trees, jolting
A leaf here or there:
So troops stand at attention,
Motionless but for eye-blinks.

ALL HALLOWS' EVE

They are not the dead,
These sheeted tykes at the door,
Asking for candy:
But they are our successors,
And we their ghostly elders.

WILD ASTERS

In the frost-quelled field,
Asters yet fly the yearning
Colors of desire.
All honor to Aaron Burr,
Whose last whisper was "*Madame . . .*"

Mayflies

In somber forest, when the sun was low,
I saw from unseen pools a mist of flies
      In their quadrillions rise
And animate a ragged patch of glow
With sudden glittering—as when a crowd
      Of stars appear
Through a brief gap in black and driven cloud,
One arc of their great round-dance showing clear.

It was no muddled swarm I witnessed, for
In *entrechats* each fluttering insect there
      Rose two steep yards in air,
Then slowly floated down to climb once more,
So that they all composed a manifold
      And figured scene,
And seemed the weavers of some cloth of gold,
Or the fine pistons of some bright machine.

[handwritten: word from ballet—]
[handwritten: Jacque D'Amboise, Susanne Farrell]

Watching those lifelong dancers of a day
As night closed in, I felt myself alone
      In a life too much my own,
More mortal in my separateness than they—
Unless, I thought, I had been called to be
      Not fly or star
But one whose task is joyfully to see
How fair the fiats of the caller are.

[handwritten: caller - does he have in mind the caller of a square-dance? Or...?]

A Short History

Corn planted us; tamed cattle made us tame.
Thence hut and citadel and kingdom came.

Fabrications

As if to prove again
The bright resilience of the frailest form,
A spider has repaired her broken web
Between the palm-trunk and the jasmine tree.

Etched on the clear new light
Above the still-imponderable ground,
It is a single and gigantic eye
Whose golden pupil, now, the spider is.

Through it you catch the flash
Of steeples brightened as a cloud slips over,
One loitering star, and off there to the south
Slow vultures kettling in the lofts of air.

Each day men frame and weave
In their own way whatever looms in sight,
Though they must see with human scale and bias,
And though there is much unseen. The Talmud tells

How dusty travelers once
Came to a river where a roc was wading,
And would have hastened then to strip and bathe,
Had not a booming voice from heaven said,

"Step not into that water:
Seven years since, a joiner dropped his axe
Therein, and it hath not yet reached the bottom."
Whether beneath our senses or beyond them,

The world is bottomless,
A drift of star-specks or the Red King's dream,
And fogs our thought, although it is not true
That we grasp nothing till we grasp it all.

Witness this ancient map
Where so much blank and namelessness surround
A little mushroom-clump of coastal towers
In which we may infer civility,

A harbor-full of spray,
And all those loves which hint of love itself,
Imagining too a pillar at whose top
A spider's web upholds the architrave.

Signatures

See p. 77

False Solomon's Seal—
So called because it lacks a
Star-scar on the heel,

And ends its arched stem
In a spray of white florets,
Later changing them

To a red, not blue,
Spatter of berries—is no
Falser than the true.

Solomon, who raised
The temple and wrote the song,
Wouldn't have dispraised

This bowed, graceful plant
So like an aspergillum,
Nor its variant

'aspergillus': any of a genus of fungi of the family Aspergillus—

With root duly scarred,
Whose bloom-hung stem is like the
Bell-branch of a bard.

? Not in my office dictionary.

Liking best to live
In the deep woods whose light is
Most contemplative,

23

Both are often found
Where mandrake, wintergreen, and
Dry leaves strew the ground,

Their heads inclining
Toward the dark earth, one blessing
And one divining.

Icons

They are one answer to the human need
For a second life, and they exist for us
In the secular heaven of photography,
    Safe in emulsion's cloud

Through which we glimpse them, knowing them as
    we know
The angels, by report and parched surmise.
Like Milton's seraphim who veil their gaze
    Against the beams of God,

Often we see them handsomely asquint
When captured by a bursting photoflash,
Or dazzling and bedazzled on that beach
    Where currently they sun;

And yet perhaps they seem most brilliant when,
Putting away all glamour, they appear
In their old clothes at home, with dog and child,
    Projecting toward the lens

From a couch not unlike our own, a smile
Sublimely confident of mattering.
They smile, too, when we spot their avatars
    Upon the actual street,

Sharing with us the little joke that we
Have known them in a different dimension;
But since they strike us then as subtly changed—
Pale, short, a trifle older—

It is not hard to yield them back to dream,
From which their images immutably
Bestow a flourish on our muted lives,
Even though death betray them.

Still, there are fewer sightings year by year
Of the trenchcoat carried niftily over the shoulder,
The innocent sultry look, the heaved guitar,
The charming pillbox hat,

And fewer of their dreamers left to grieve
As all those glossy selves, transcendent still,
Slip unaccountably into the morgues
And archives of this world.

Crow's Nests

That lofty stand of trees beyond the field,
Which in the storms of summer stood revealed

As a great fleet of galleons bound our way
Across a moiled expanse of tossing hay,

Full-rigged and swift, and to the topmost sail
Taking their fill and pleasure of the gale,

Now, in this leafless time, are ships no more,
Though it would not be hard to take them for

A roadstead full of naked mast and spar
In which we see now where the crow's nests are.

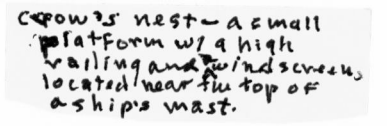

crow's nest — a small
platform w/ a high
railing and windscreen,
located near the top of
a ship's mast.

STÉPHANE MALLARMÉ: **Sea Breeze**

The flesh grows weary. And books, I've read them all.
Off, then, to where I glimpse through spray and squall
Strange birds delighting in their unknown skies!
No antique gardens mirrored in my eyes
Can stay my sea-changed spirit, nor the light
Of my abstracted lamp which shines (O Night!)
On the guardian whiteness of the empty sheet,
Nor the young wife who gives the babe her teat.
Come, ship whose masts now gently rock and sway,
Raise anchor for a stranger world! Away!

How strange that Boredom, all its hopes run dry,
Still dreams of handkerchiefs that wave good-bye!
Those gale-inviting masts might creak and bend
In seas where many a craft has met its end,
Dismasted, lost, with no green island near it...
But hear the sailors singing, O my spirit!

from the French

29

NINA CASSIAN: **Ballad of the Jack of Diamonds**

Here is the Jack of Diamonds, clad
In the rusty coat he's always had.
His two dark brothers wish him dead,
As does the third, whose hue is red.

Here is the Jack of Diamonds, whom
The fates have marked for certain doom.
He is a mediocre fellow,
A scrawny jack whose chest is hollow
And spattered with a dismal yellow—
No model for a Donatello.

The two dark brothers of this jack,
Abetted by the third, alack,
(Who, draped in hearts from head to foot,
Is the most knavish of the lot),
Have vowed by all means to be free
Of him who gives them symmetry,
Making a balanced set of four
Whose equilibrium they abhor.

One brother, on his breast and sleeves,
Is decked with tragic, spadelike leaves.
The next has crosses for décor.
The motif of the third is gore.

The Jack of Diamonds is dead,
Leaving a vacuum in his stead.

This ballad seems at least twice-told.
Well, all Romanian plots are old.

from the Romanian

Once

The old rock-climber cries out in his sleep,
    Dreaming without enthusiasm
Of a great cliff immeasurably steep,
        Or of the sort of yawning chasm,
            Now far too deep,
That once, made safe by rashness, he could leap.

casuarina — any tree of the genus *Casuarina*, native to Australia + SE Asia, having the scale-leaves on slender jointed branches, resembling gigantic horsetails.

croton — any small tree or shrub of the genus *Croton*, with colored ornamental leaves.

Bone Key see p. 78

> He used to call his body Brother Ass...
> St. Bonaventure, *Life of St. Francis*

You would think that here, at least,
In dens by night, on tawny sands by day,
Poor Brother Ass would be a kingly beast.
So does the casuarina seem to say,

Whose kindred haziness
Of head is flattering to a bloodshot eye;
So too the palm's blown shadows, which caress
Anointed brows and bodies where they lie,

And angel's-trumpets, which
Proclaim a musky scent in fleshly tones.
Yet in this island soil, that's only rich
In rock and coral and Calusa bones,

It's hardihood that thrives,
As when a screw pine that the gale has downed,
Shooting new prop-roots from its trunk, survives
In bristling disarray by change of ground,

Or the white mangrove, nursed
In sea-soaked earth and air, contrives to expel
From leafstalk glands the salt with which it's cursed,
Or crotons, scorched as by the flames of Hell,

          Protectively attire
Their leaves in leather, and so move to and fro
In the hot drafts that stir the sun's harsh fire,
Like Shadrach, Meshach, and Abednego.

Personae

1

The poet, mindful of the daring lives
Of bards who dwelt in garrets, drank in dives,
And bought in little shops within the means
Of working folk their soup-bone, salt, and beans,
Becoming, in the cause of literature,
Adjunctive members of the laboring poor,

Ascends the platform now to read his verse
Dressed like a sandhog, stevedore, or worse,
And wears a collar of memorial blue
To give the brave Bohemian past its due.

2

Musicians, who remember when their sort
Were hirelings at some duke's or prince's court,
Obliged to share the noble patron's feast
Belowstairs, or below the salt at least,
Now sweep onto the concert stage disguised
As those by whom they once were patronized.

How princely are their tailcoats! How refined
Their airs, their gracious gestures! And behind
The great conductor who urbanely bows
Rise rank on rank on rank of noble brows.

VALERI PETROV: **A Cry from Childhood**

Why must it come just now to trouble me,
This sudden, shrill, and dreamlike cry
Of children calling "Valeri! Valeri!"
Out in the street nearby?

It is not for me, that distant childhood call;
Alas, it is for me no more.
They are calling now to someone else, my small
Namesake who lives next door.

Though such disturbances, I must admit,
Are troubling to my train of thought,
I keep my feelings to myself, for it
Would be comical, would it not,

If, from his high and studious retreat,
A gaunt old man leaned out to say
"I can't come out" to the children in the street,
"I'm not allowed to play."

from the Bulgarian

VALERI PETROV: **Photos from the Archives**

Those manly brows, those eyes so steady,
Those mouths unwilling to betray,
And under them those thin necks, ready
To wear a gallows-rope next day:

Old Nazi archives saved for us
These pictures of our friends who died.
Mug shots, we know, look always thus,
Full face and profile, side by side,

Yet sometimes guilty thoughts arise
Which make us fancy that these men
Have looked once deep into our eyes,
And turned their faces from us then.

from the Bulgarian

A Digression

Having confided to the heavy-lipped
Mailbox his great synoptic manuscript,
He stands light-headed in the lingering clang.
How lightly, too, he feels his briefcase hang!

And now it swings beside his knees, as they
From habit start him on his evening way,
With the tranced rhythm of a metronome,
Past hall and grove and stadium toward his home.

Yet as the sun-bathed campus slips behind,
A giddy lack of purpose fills his mind,
Making him swerve into a street which for
Two decades he has managed to ignore.

What stops him in his tracks is that his soul,
Proposing nothing, innocent of goal,
Sees no perspective narrowing between
Gold-numbered doors and frontages of green,

But for the moment an obstructive storm
Of specks and flashes that will take no form,
A roiled mosaic or a teeming scrim
That seems to have no pertinence to him.

(over)

scrim — Theater: the loosely woven fabric used in a theater as a transparent drop.

It is his purpose now as, turning 'round,
He takes his bearings and is homeward bound,
To ponder what the world's confusion meant
When he regarded it without intent.

A Wall in the Woods: Cummington

1

What is it for, now that dividing neither
Farm from farm nor field from field, it runs
Through deep impartial woods, and is transgressed
By boughs of pine or beech from either side?
Under that woven tester, buried here
Or there in laurel-patch or shrouding vine,
It is for grief at what has come to nothing,
What even in this hush is scarcely heard—
Whipcrack, the ox's lunge, the stoneboat's grating,
Work-shouts of young men stooped before their time
Who in their stubborn heads foresaw forever
The rose of apples and the blue of rye.
It is for pride, as well, in pride that built
With levers, tackle, and abraded hands
What two whole centuries have not brought down.
Look how with shims they made the stones weigh
        inward,
Binding the water-rounded with the flat;
How to a small ravine they somehow lugged
A long, smooth girder of a rock, on which
To launch their wall in air, and overpass
The narrow stream that still slips under it.
Rosettes of lichen decorate their toils,
Who labored here like Pharaoh's Israelites;
Whose grandsons left for Canaans in the west.
Except to prompt a fit of elegy

tester – a canopy,
esp over a four
poster bed

It is for us no more, or if it is,
It is a sort of music for the eye,
A rugged ground bass like the bagpipe's drone
On which the leaf-light like a chanter plays.

2
He will hear no guff ✶
About Jamshýd's court, this small,
Striped, duff-colored resident
On top of the wall,

Who, having given
An apotropaic ✶✶ shriek
Echoed by crows in heaven,
Is off like a streak.

There is no tracing
The leaps and scurries with which
He braids his long castle, ra-
Cing, by gap, ledge, niche

And Cyclopean
Passages, to reappear
Sentry-like on a rampart
Thirty feet from here.

What is he saying
Now, in a steady chipping
Succinctly plucked and cadenced
As water dripping?

✶ in The Rubyat of Oman Kyam
✶✶ apotropaic ~ intended to avent evil influence
apo - Greek: off, from, away, quite.

chanter — the melody-
pipe, with finger holes,
of a bag-pipe

It is not drum-taps
For a lost race of giants,
But perhaps says something, here
In Mr. Bryant's

Homiletic woods,
Of the brave art of forage
And the good of a few nuts
In burrow-storage;

Of agility
That is not sorrow's captive,
Lost as it is in being
Briskly adaptive;

Of the plenum, charged
With one life through all changes,
And of how we are enlarged
By what estranges.

William Cullen Bryant - (To a Waterfowl) pub in New Ox-
ford Book
of Amer-
ican Verse

plenum - a condition of fullness; a full assembly, all members present.

❦ Elsewhere

The delectable names of harsh places:
Cilicia* Aspera, Estremadura.
In that smooth wave of cello-sound, Mojave,
We hear no ill of brittle parch and glare.

So late October's pasture-fringe,
With aster-blur and ferns of toasted gold,
Invites to barrens where the crop to come
Is stone prized upward by the deepening freeze.

Speechless and cold the stars arise
On the small garden where we have dominion.
Yet in three tongues we speak of Taurus' name
And of Aldebaran and the Hyades,*

Recalling what at best we know,
That there is beauty bleak and far from ours,
Great reaches where the Lord's delighting mind,
Though not inhuman, ponders other things.

ncient district in *atolia, now in S.* *rkey*

* Group of stars near the Pleiades, in constellation Taurus

49

CHARLES BAUDELAIRE: **The Albatross**

Often, for pastime, mariners will ensnare
The albatross, that vast sea-bird who sweeps
On high companionable pinion where
Their vessel glides upon the bitter deeps.

Torn from his native space, this captive king
Flounders upon the deck in stricken pride,
And pitiably lets his great white wing
Drag like a heavy paddle at his side.

This rider of winds, how awkward he is, and weak!
How droll he seems, who was all grace of late!
A sailor pokes a pipestem into his beak;
Another, hobbling, mocks his trammeled gait.

The Poet is like this monarch of the clouds,
Familiar of storms, of stars, and of all high things;
Exiled on earth amidst its hooting crowds,
He cannot walk, borne down by giant wings.

from the French

CHARLES BAUDELAIRE: **Correspondences**

Nature's a temple whose living colonnades
Breathe forth a mystic speech in fitful sighs;
Man wanders among symbols in those glades,
Where all things watch him with familiar eyes.

Like dwindling echoes gathered far away
Into a deep and thronging unison
Huge as the night or as the light of day,
All scents and sounds and colors meet as one.

Perfumes there are as sweet as the oboe's sound,
Green as the prairies, fresh as a child's caress,
—And there are others, rich, corrupt, profound

And of an infinite pervasiveness,
Like myrrh, or musk, or amber, that excite
The ecstasies of sense, the soul's delight.

from the French

This Pleasing Anxious Being

see p. 78 (line from
"Tray's Elegy Written etc."
Oxford Book of English
Verse pp 278 - 281.
Quoted line on p 280.

1

In no time you are back where safety was,
Spying upon the lambent table where
Good family faces drink the candlelight
As in a manger scene by de La Tour.   — L.A. County Museum
Father has finished carving at the sideboard   has one, And
And Mother's hand has touched a little bell,   Getty?
So that, beside her chair, Roberta looms
With serving bowls of yams and succotash.
When will they speak, or stir? They wait for you
To recollect that, while it lived, the past
Was a rushed present, fretful and unsure.
The muffled clash of silverware begins,
With ghosts of gesture, with a laugh retrieved,
And the warm, edgy voices you would hear:
Rest for a moment in that resonance.
But see your small feet kicking under the table,
Fiercely impatient to be off and play.

2

The shadow of whoever took the picture
Reaches like Azrael's across the sand
Toward grown-ups blithe in black and white, encamped
Where surf behind them floods a rocky cove.
They turn with wincing smiles, shielding their eyes
Against the sunlight and the future's glare,
Which notes their bathing caps, their quaint maillots, French: a
The wicker picnic hamper then in style, tight-filling, one-
And will convict them of mortality. piece swimsuit.
Two boys, however, do not plead with time,
Distracted as they are by what?—perhaps
A whacking flash of gull-wings overhead—
While off to one side, with his back to us,
A painter, perched before his easel, seeing
The marbled surges come to various ruin,
Seeks out of all those waves to build a wave
That shall in blue summation break forever.

Azrael: in the Koran, angel of death: severs soul
from body. Name and concept borrowed
from Judaism.

3

Wild, lashing snow, which thumps against the
    windshield
Like earth tossed down upon a coffin-lid,
Half clogs the wipers, and our Buick yaws
On the black roads of 1928.
Father is driving; Mother, leaning out,
Tracks with her flashlight beam the pavement's edge,
And we must weather hours more of storm
To be in Baltimore for Christmastime.
Of the two children in the back seat, safe
Beneath a lap-robe, soothed by jingling chains
And by their parents' pluck and gaiety,
One is asleep. The other's half-closed eyes
Make out at times the dark hood of the car
Ploughing the eddied flakes, and might foresee
The steady chugging of a landing craft
Through morning mist to the bombarded shore,
Or a deft prow that dances through the rocks
In the white water of the Allagash,
Or, in good time, the bedstead at whose foot
The world will swim and flicker and be gone.

Transformations

The Prologue to Molière's *Amphitryon*

See pp. 78 - 79
(title shld have given us the page numbers here.)

Mercury, on a cloud: Night, in a chariot drawn through the air by two horses

MERCURY   Whoa, charming Night! I beg you, stop and tarry.
There is a favor I would ask of you.
      I bring you a word or two
      As Jupiter's emissary.

NIGHT   So it's you, Lord Mercury! Heaven knows,
I scarcely knew you in that languid pose!

MERCURY   Ah me! I was so weary and so lame
From running errands at great Jove's behest,
I sat down on a little cloud to rest
      And wait until you came.

NIGHT   Oh, come now, Mercury. Is it proper for
A god to say that he is tired and sore?

MERCURY   Are we made of iron?

NIGHT   No; but we must maintain
A tone befitting our divinity.
Some words, if uttered by the gods, profane
      Our lofty rank and high degree,
      And such base language ought to be
      Restricted to the human plane.

MERCURY   That's easy enough for you to say;
                You have, my sweet, a chariot and a pair
                Of splendid steeds to whisk you everywhere
                In a most nonchalant and queenly way.
                    But my life's not like that at all;
                And, given my unjust and dismal fate,
                    I owe the poets endless hate
                    For their unutterable gall
                    In having heartlessly decreed,
                    Ever since Homer sang of Troy,
                    That each god, for his use and need,
                    Should have a chariot to enjoy,
                    While I must go on foot, indeed,
                    Like some mere village errand-boy—
                I, who in heaven and on earth am known
                As the famed messenger of Jove's high throne,
                    And who, without exaggeration,
                    Considering all the chores I'm given,
                    Need, more than anyone in Heaven,
                    To have some decent transportation.

NIGHT   Too bad, but there's no help for it;
                The poets treat us as they please.
                There's no end to the idiocies
                That those fine gentlemen commit.
           Still, you are wrong to chide them so severely;
                They gave you wingèd heels; that's quite a gift.

MERCURY   Oh, yes: they've made my feet more swift,
                But does that make my legs less weary?

NIGHT   Lord Mercury, your point is made.
                Now, what's this message that you bear?

MERCURY   It comes from Jove, as you're aware.
He wishes you to cloak him with your shade
  While, in a gallant escapade,
  He consummates a new affair.
To you, Jove's habits can be nothing new;
You know how often he forsakes the skies;
How much he likes to put on human guise
When there are mortal beauties to pursue,
  And how he's full of tricks and lies
  That purest maids have yielded to.
Alcmena's bright eyes lately turned his head;
And while, upon the far Boeotian plain,
  Amphitryon, her lord, has led
  His Thebans in a fierce campaign,
Jove's taken his form and, acting in his stead,
  Is eased now of his amorous pain
By the soft pleasures of the lady's bed.
It serves his purpose that the couple were
But lately married; and the youthful heat
Of their amours, their ardor keen and sweet,
Were what inclined the crafty Jupiter
  To this particular deceit.
His tactic has succeeded, in this case:
  Though, doubtless, such impersonations
Would, with most wives, be vain and out of place;
It isn't always that her husband's face
  Will give a woman palpitations.

NIGHT Jove baffles me, and I have trouble seeing
Why these impostures give him such delight.

MERCURY He likes to sample every state of being,
And in so doing he's divinely right.

65

However high the role that men assign him,
    I'd not think much of him if he
Forever played the awesome deity
And let the jeweled bounds of Heaven confine him.
It is, I think, the height of silly pride
Always to be imprisoned in one's splendor;
Above all, if one would enjoy the tender
Passions, one must set one's rank aside.
Jove is a connoisseur of pleasures, who
Is practiced in descending from on high;
When he would enter into any new
    Delight, he lays his selfhood by,
And Jupiter the god is lost to view.

NIGHT   One might excuse his leaving our high station
To mix with mankind in a lower place,
And sample human passions, however base,
    And share men's foolish agitation,
If only, in his taste for transformation,
He'd join no species save the human race.
    But for great Jupiter to change
    Into a bull, or swan, or snake,
    Is most unsuitable and strange,
And causes tongues to cluck and heads to shake.

MERCURY   Let critics carp, in their conceit:
    Such metamorphoses are sweet
    In ways they cannot comprehend.
Jove knows what he's about, in all his dealings;
And in their passions and their tender feelings,
Brutes are less brutish than some folk contend.

NIGHT Let us revert to the current lady-friend.
     If Jove's sly trick has proved auspicious,
     What does he ask of me? What more can he need?

MERCURY That you rein in your horses, check their speed,
     And thereby satisfy his amorous wishes,
       Stretching a night that's most delicious
       Into a night that's long indeed;
     That you allow his fires more time to burn,
     And stave the daylight off, lest it awaken
       The man whose place he's taken,
       And hasten his return.

NIGHT   It's not the prettiest of tasks
       That Jupiter would have me do!
       There's a sweet name for creatures who
       Perform the service that he asks!

MERCURY   For a young goddess, you embrace
       Old-fashioned notions, it seems to me;
       To do such service isn't base
       Except in those of low degree.
     When one is blessed with high estate and standing,
       All that one does is good as gold,
       And things have different names, depending
       On what position one may hold.

NIGHT   In matters of this dubious kind
       You've more experience than I;
       I'll trust your counsel, then, and try
       To do this thing that Jove's assigned.

MERCURY   Ho! Dearest Madam Night, take care;
Don't overdo it, pray; go easy.
Your reputation everywhere
Is not for being prim and queasy.
In every clime, you've played a shady part
In many a tryst and rendezvous;
As far as morals are concerned, dear heart,
There's little to choose between us two.

NIGHT   Enough. Let's cease to bicker thus;
Let us maintain our dignities,
And let's not prompt mankind to laugh at us
By too much frankness, if you please.

MERCURY Farewell. I must descend now, right away,
And, putting off the form of Mercury,
So change that I may seem to be
Amphitryon's valet.

NIGHT   I shall ride on but, as you ask of me,
I'll often dawdle and delay.

MERCURY Good day, dear Night.

NIGHT   Good Mercury, good day.

DANTE ALIGHIERI: **Canto XXV of the *Inferno***

see p. 79

The thief, when he had done with prophecy,
  made figs of both his lifted hands, and cried,
  "Take these, O God, for they are aimed at Thee!"

Then was my heart upon the serpents' side,
  for 'round his neck one coiled like a garrote
  as if to say, "Enough of ranting pride,"

And another pinned his arms, and tied a knot
  of head and tail in front of him again,
  so tightly that they could not stir one jot.

Alas, Pistoia, why dost thou not ordain
  that thou be burnt to ashes, since thou hast
  out-sinned the base begetters of thy strain?

In the dark rounds of Hell through which I passed,
  I saw no spirit so blaspheme his Lord,
  not him who from the Theban wall was cast.

He fled then, speaking not another word,
  and into sight a raging centaur came:
  "Where has that half-cooked sinner gone?" he
   roared.

So many snakes Maremma cannot claim
      as covered all his back in dense array,
      to where his form took on a human frame.

Behind his nape, upon his shoulders, lay
      a seething dragon with its wings outspread,
      which sets afire whatever comes its way.

"Him you behold is Cacus," my master said,
      "who underneath the rock of the Aventine
      so often made a lake of bloody red.

He is not with his brothers, since condign
      justice has set him here, who to his den
      so craftily made off with Geryon's kine:

For that, his crooked ways were ended then
      by the club of Hercules, which dealt him nigh
      a hundred blows, of which he felt not ten."

While thus he spoke, the centaur hastened by,
      and from below three spirits came in view,
      whose coming neither my great guide nor I

Perceived until they shouted, "Who are you?"
      At that, we two broke off our talk together
      and turned our whole attention to that crew.

Who they might be I did not promptly gather;
      but, as may chance in meetings of the kind,
      one had occasion then to name another,

Saying, "Where's Cianfa? Why did he fall behind?"
  I put my finger to my lips, to show
  my guide that he should wait and pay them mind.

'Twill be no wonder, Reader, if you are slow
  to trust the thing that I shall now impart,
  for I, who saw it, scarce believe it so.

I watched a vile, six-footed serpent dart
  toward one of them, and then, with never a
    pause,
  fasten itself to him with every part.

It clasped his belly with its middle claws,
  its forefeet clutched his arms as in a vise,
  and into either cheek it sank its jaws.

The hindmost feet it dug into his thighs,
  and twixt them thrust its tail so limberly
  that up his spine its clambering tip could rise.

Never did ivy cling so to a tree
  as did that hideous creature bind and braid
  its limbs and his in pure ferocity;

And then they stuck together, as if made
  of melting wax, and mixed their colors; nor
  did either now retain his former shade;

Just so, when paper burns, there runs before
  the creeping flame a stain of darkish hue
  that, though not black as yet, is white no more.

The other two cried out to him they knew,
      saying, "Agnello, how you change! Ah me,
      already you are neither one nor two."

The two heads now were one, and we could see
      two faces fuse in one blear visage, where
      no vestiges of either seemed to be.

Four forelimbs now combined to make a pair
      of arms, and strange new members grew in place
      of the bellies, legs, and chests that had been there.

Their erstwhile shapes were gone without a trace,
      and the monstrous form that was and was not they
      now moved away with slow and stumbling pace.

As lizards, in the cruelest heat of day,
      skitter from hedge to hedge along a lane,
      and flash like lightning if they cross the way,

So, toward the bellies of the other twain,
      there sped a little reptile, fiery-hot
      and blackly glinting as a pepper-grain:

It now transfixed, in one of them, the spot
      through which our earliest nourishment must
         come;
      then fell, and sprawled before him like a sot.

The victim gazed at it, and yet was dumb;
      he stood stock-still, and did but yawn a bit,
      as if some drowsy fever made him numb.

The serpent looked on him, and he on it;
      from the one's mouth and the other's wound, a
         spate
      of smoke poured out, and the fumes converged
      and knit.

Of poor Sabellus' and Nasidius' fate
      let Lucan tell no more, but listen now
      to what I saw. Let Ovid not relate

Of Cadmus and of Arethusa, how
      they turned to snake or fountain by his grace;
      no envy of those feats need I avow,

For he never made two creatures, face to face,
      so change that each one let the other seize
      its very substance, as in the present case.

Incited by their mutual sympathies,
      the serpent caused its tail now to divide,
      and the wretch pressed together his feet and
         knees.

His legs and thighs adhered then, side to side,
      soon blending, so that nowhere, low or high,
      could any seam or juncture be descried.

The cloven tail took on the form that by
      degrees the other lost, and now its skin
      turned soft, while the other's hardened in reply.

I saw the armpits of the man begin
    to engulf the arms, while the beast's short forelegs
        grew
    by just that length to which the arms sank in.

Its two hind feet entwined, and turned into
    that member which by mankind is concealed,
    and the thief's one member branched then into
        two.

Now, while the smoke by which they both were veiled
    transposed their hues, and planted on one crown
    the hair that from the other it plucked and
        peeled,

The one arose, the other toppled down,
    and each, still grimly staring, set about
    to make the other's lineaments his own.

The upright one drew back his upper snout,
    and from his brow the excess matter ran
    downward, till from the cheeks two ears grew
        out;

Then the nether remnant of the snout began,
    out of its superfluity, to make
    a human nose, and the full lips of a man.

The prone one thrust his jaws out like a snake,
    and at the same time drew his ears inside,
    as a snail retracts its horns for safety's sake,

And cleft his tongue, that once was unified
    and shaped for speech. Then, in the other's head,
    the forked tongue healed, and the smoke could
      now subside.

The soul that had become a beast now fled
    hissing away; the other, who had begun
    to speak in sputters, followed where it led,

Yet turned his new-made shoulders toward the one
    who lingered, saying, "Buoso shall crawl through
      this
    stony terrain awhile, as I have done."

Thus did the cargo of the seventh abyss
    change and re-change; let the strangeness of it,
      pray,
    excuse me if my pen has gone amiss.

Although my thoughts were fuddled by dismay
    and my eyes a bit uncertain, all the same
    those darkling spirits did not steal away

Ere I knew one for Puccio, called the Lame;
    and he had been the only one to keep
    his form, of the three thieves who earlier came.

The other was he, Gaville, who made thee weep.

Notes

Zea The title is one half of the botanical name (*Zea mays*) for Indian corn or maize.

At Moorditch In act 1, scene 2, of *Henry the Fourth, Part I,* Prince Hal says to Falstaff, "What sayest thou to a hare, or the melancholy of Moor Ditch?" Moorditch seemed to me a good name for the sort of hospital where people are treated for depression.

Signatures Gerard's *Herball* (1597) says of Solomon's Seal that "The root is white and thicke, full of knobs or joints, in some places resembling the mark of a seale, whereof I thinke it tooke the name *Sigillum Solomonis.*" Evidently some herbalists saw in the "raised orbicular scars of the stems of former years" (Homer D. House, *Wild Flowers*) a pattern resembling the magical five-pointed or six-pointed star called Solomon's Seal. The rootstock of False Solomon's Seal also bears the scars of former stems, but no such pattern has been discerned in them. Yeats's poems mention more than once the bell-branch which was the insignia of the ancient Celtic bard or ollave. And Robert Graves, in his *White Goddess,* tells of "the branch of golden bells which were the ollave's emblem of office."

Bone Key The name "Key West" comes from Spanish "Cayo Hueso" (Bone Island), which may or may not derive from intertribal Indian warfare, the final massacre of the Calusas, and the littering of the island with their bones. The casuarina, a feathery tree that takes its name from the cassowary bird, has an aptitude for growing in seacoast sand and is also known as Australian pine. Angel's-trumpet is a poisonous, narcotic tree of the genus *Datura*. Screw pine is a common name for the large Asiatic shrub pandanus. White mangroves and crotons are well-known, and so, surely, are Shadrach, Meshach, and Abednego.

A Wall in the Woods: Cummington Jamshýd, a legendary king of ancient Persia, is mentioned in an *ubi sunt* manner by FitzGerald's Omar Khayyám: "They say the Lion and the Lizard keep / The courts where Jamshýd gloried and drank deep." William Cullen Bryant (1794–1878), whose poems often found lessons in nature, was born and raised in Cummington, Massachusetts, and returned there in his latter years.

This Pleasing Anxious Being The title is taken from the twenty-second stanza of Thomas Gray's "Elegy Written in a Country Churchyard."

The Prologue to Molière's *Amphitryon* Molière's three-act comedy *Amphitryon* (1668) was based on a Latin tragicomedy of the second century B.C., the *Amphitruo* of Plautus, and was influenced as well by Jean de Rotrou's prior French adaptation, *Les Sosies* (1636). It is generally agreed that Molière greatly improved upon

his sources. In any case, the prologue is wholly
Molière's idea and owes nothing to any earlier play.
The form of the prologue, and that of the play as a
whole, is the system of *vers libres* which Molière's
friend La Fontaine was then employing for his *Fables*:
in writing *vers libres,* one is free at any moment to alter
line length or rhyme pattern for expressive reasons.

Dante Alighieri: Canto XXV of the *Inferno* This
translation was done for Daniel Halpern's *Dante's
Inferno: Translations by Twenty Contemporary Poets* ~~Seems a bad idea.~~
(Ecco, 1993). Of my notes, included in the Ecco
volume and much indebted to such scholars as Charles
Singleton, I give here the summarizing first paragraph.

*Dante and Virgil are still in the Seventh Chasm, to which
the souls of thieves are assigned. As Canto XXIV has shown,
it is a dark place, and full of reptiles that variously punish
the sinners—twining around them so as to bind their
thievish hands, or (as happened to Vanni Fucci in XXIV)
causing them to burn to ashes and then re-form. What
first occurs in Canto XXV is that Vanni Fucci, at the
conclusion of a prophecy grievous to Dante, makes a
gesture of obscene defiance toward God, is therefore
throttled and bound by serpents, and flees, pursued by the* ??
*centaur Cacus. The remainder of the canto is concerned
with the transformations undergone by five thieves of
Florence, all of noble family, who have been identified as
Agnello de' Brunelleschi, Buoso (degli Abati?), Puccio
"Sciancato" de' Galigai, Cianfa de' Donati, and Francesco
de' Cavalcanti. Cianfa, who has been changed into a six-
footed serpent, attacks Agnello and merges with him to
create a monster that is neither reptile nor man. Then*

Francesco, who is temporarily a small reptile, assaults Buoso and exchanges shapes with him, the man becoming a serpentello *and the reptile becoming a man. Puccio remains unchanged, but for the moment only. The logic of these painful transformations is that the thieves, who in life appropriated what was not theirs, are here punished by the repeated loss even of their own persons.*